Passing the PRINCE2 Examinations

Ken Bradley

London: TSO

Published by TSO (The Stationery Office) and available from:

Online
www.tso.co.uk/bookshop

Mail, Telephone, Fax & E-mail
TSO
PO Box 29, Norwich NR3 1GN
Telephone orders/General enquiries 0870 600 5522
Fax orders 0870 600 5533
Email book.orders@tso.co.uk
Textphone 0870 240 3701

TSO Shops
123 Kingsway, London WC2B 6PQ
020 7242 6393 Fax 020 7242 6394
68-69 Bull Street, Birmingham B4 6AD
0121 236 9696 Fax 0121 236 9699
9-21 Princess Street, Manchester M60 8AS
0161 834 7201 Fax 0161 833 0634
16 Arthur Street, Belfast BT1 4GD
028 9023 8451 Fax 028 9023 5401
18-19 High Street, Cardiff CF10 1PT
029 2039 5548 Fax 029 2038 4347
71 Lothian Road, Edinburgh EH3 9AZ
0870 606 5566 Fax 0870 606 5588

TSO Accredited Agents
(See Yellow Pages)

and through good booksellers

The information contained in this publication is believed to be correct at the time of manufacture. Whilst care has been taken to ensure that the information is accurate, the publisher can accept no responsibility for any errors or omissions or for changes to the details given.

A CIP catalogue record for this book is available from the British Library
A Library of Congress CIP catalogue record has been applied for

First published 2002
Fourth impression 2004

ISBN 0 11 330912 0

Printed in the United Kingdom by The Stationery Office
ID 168285 04/04 C50 19585 960951

Contents

Foreword

This book is aimed at easing the path for all those intending to take the APM Group PRINCE2 foundation and practitioner examinations. Those taking the APM Group Practitioner Re-Registration Examination will find that the advice provided is equally relevant and useful. *Passing the PRINCE2 Examinations* has been updated to reflect changes to the PRINCE2 reference manual released early in 2002.

Thanks go to examiners Sheila Roberts and Colin Bentley for taking on most of the hard work relating to the examination question examples. Also to the APM Group and the PRINCE2 Examination Board for allowing the use of PRINCE2 examination material, and Richard Pharro for his support and encouragement in getting this publication to print.

I hope you will find this book of real use in preparing for, and passing, your examinations. The royalties from this book go to the APM Group annual PRINCE2 award scheme – full details of which can be obtained from the APM Group.

Ken Bradley

February 2002

The Foundation Examination

What is the examination?

The Foundation Examination is a one-hour, closed-book examination. It is designed to test the candidate's knowledge of the PRINCE2 method by choosing the correct answer from a selection of possible answers. There are 75 questions in all and candidates must score 38 correct answers or more to pass. There is no consolidation or carry-forward of time or scores to the Practitioner Examination – the Foundation Examination stands alone. Candidates intending to take the PRINCE2 Practitioner Examination (or any other PRINCE-related examination) must first pass the Foundation Examination.

The track record

Statistics released by the APM Group to PRINCE2 Accredited Training Organisations (ATOs) show that around 95% of all candidates pass the Foundation Examination indicating that the level of understanding of the PRINCE2 method, usually achieved following an accredited training event, is high.

Only around 65% of candidates taking the Registered Practitioner Examination reach the required standard, indicating that their ability to take a project scenario and answer questions with reference to the PRINCE2 method, thereby demonstrating they are able to apply the Method to a practical situation, is comparatively low. A later section of this publication provides advice and guidance on the Practitioner Examination.

There is an interesting correlation between marks scored in the Foundation Examination and success in the Practitioner Examination – essentially the more marks scored in the Foundation Examination, the higher the success rate at practitioner level. Candidates who pass the Foundation Examination with 38–40 marks are, statistically, much less likely to pass the Practitioner Examination; those with Foundation Examination scores in excess of 70 marks almost always pass the Practitioner Examination. This is why many accredited training courses focus mainly on the content of the PRINCE2 method for most of the event.

The examination questions

On the following pages are examples of the questions and multiple choice answers that make up the Foundation Examination. Do not approach the questions 'cold'; you must have done quite a bit of preparation before attempting any, otherwise you will get demoralised!

There are over 250 questions in the APM Group database from which the actual examination questions are taken. Some of the questions are very straightforward and will give you little trouble; others drill down into the method and are there to really test your knowledge. You will find that some of the possible answers posed can be eliminated with even a basic knowledge of the method.

Preparing for the examination

Success in the Foundation Examination requires a good understanding of what makes up the PRINCE2 method and the flows of information within it. The official PRINCE2 manual (*Managing Successful Projects with PRINCE2* ISBN: 0 11 330891 4), produced by the Office of Government Commerce (OGC), does not contain a single overall, detailed process map and it is well worth producing one as part of your preparation for the examination.

The approach is to take each of the major processes (excluding 'Planning' which has multiple links to most of the other processes) and map the flows of information and products between them to produce a diagram along the following lines.

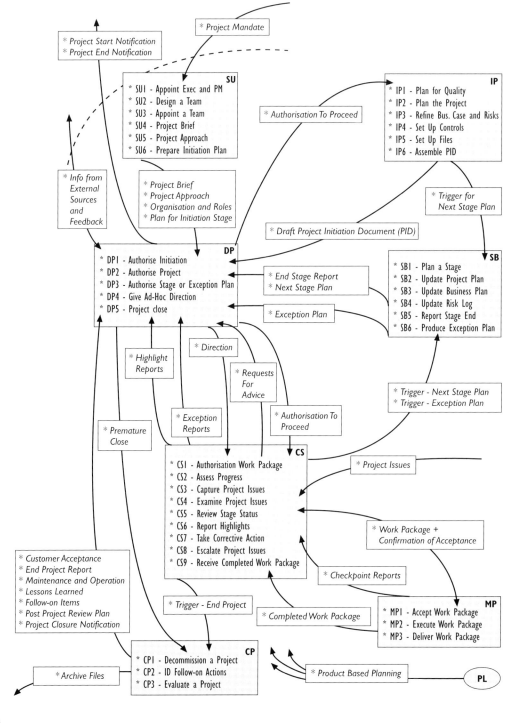

The Planning (PL) Process may be treated as a 'backdrop' to the other seven major processes, providing the required planning input as required; alternatively include the PL Process as shown in the diagram.

To get the most out of this work, a breakdown of each major process into its sub-processes is recommended to show the specific 'to and from' relationships between the processes. If you do this, your final process map will be considerably more detailed than the one shown and you might find it easier to select a new sheet for each process. Always produce your own diagram – do not rely on the one shown here!

Remember that the main benefit from creating your summary Process Diagram will come from the research you will need to do into each process. You will not be allowed to take your summary Process Diagram into the Foundation Examination but it will be a useful revision aid and helpful in structuring the content of the Practitioner Examination answers.

Technique for completing the examination

The best technique for the Foundation Examination is to go through the paper in an initial non-stop 'sweep', answering all the straightforward questions to which you know the answers; ignore any long, wordy questions or those that might need some working out (i.e. double-negative questions). The examiners are fond of including 'negative' questions (i.e. *'Which of the following is NOT …'*) and you might find it easier to return to these at a later time.

When your first sweep is completed you should have most of the questions answered; typically this will take about 25–35 minutes. You can at this stage count up the number of questions you know you have answered correctly to provide a confidence boost – but be sure this will not have the opposite effect!

Now return to those more obscure or difficult questions. Many will not be as tricky as they first appeared and, with a bit of common sense and eradication of the obvious non-starter answers, you should be able to pick up most of the marks.

Beware of changing answers you already have – general experience indicates that about two-thirds of changes made to Foundation Examination answers are changes from correct to incorrect! If you need to make a change, show it clearly – if you are attending an accredited training course the paper will be marked by the approved trainer running the event so clarity is all that is required.

You should now be ready to try a Foundation Examination paper – if you have done your preparation work you should be feeling quite confident and ready to tackle the example examination which starts on the next page. Always plan your approach to the real examination – time the completion of the example paper that follows for no more than two days before the examination – you will then be finely honed – with just enough time to review the elements you missed out on but not too much time to cause you to lose the cutting edge you'll need for the real thing.

Good luck!

The Professional Examinations

Date: ....

Foundation Examination Paper

Multiple Choice

Instructions

---

1   All 75 questions should be attempted

2   There are no trick questions

3   All answers are to be marked on the original examination paper

4   Please use a pen to mark your answers with either a ✓ or ✗. There is only one correct answer per question unless more than one is specified for that question

5   You have 1 hour for this paper

6   You must get 50% (38 or more questions) correct to pass

Candidate Number: ....

1:   Which of the following is NOT a PRINCE2 component?

   a)   Configuration Management   ☐

   b)   Business Case   ☐

   c)   Work Package   ☐

   d)   Organisation   ☐

   e)   Plans   ☐

2:   The majority of PRINCE2 controls may be described as:

   a)   Technique-based   ☐

   b)   Process-driven   ☐

   c)   Business Case-driven   ☐

   d)   Ad-hoc   ☐

   e)   Event-based   ☐

3:   In terms of a Product Breakdown Structure, what type of product is the Issue Log?

   a)   A Specialist Product   ☐

   b)   A Management Product   ☐

   c)   A Technical Product   ☐

   d)   None of these   ☐

4:   What role should check that a product is ready for a Quality Review?

   a)   The Chairman   ☐

   b)   The Producer   ☐

   c)   The Project Manager   ☐

   d)   The Reviewers   ☐

   e)   Project Support   ☐

5:   Who should ensure that tolerance is set for the project?

   a)   The Executive   ☐

   b)   The Project Board   ☐

   c)   The Senior User   ☐

   d)   The Project Manager   ☐

6:    Does PRINCE2 recommend a minimum number of stages? If so
      what is the recommendation?

      a)   One   ☐

      b)   Two   ☐

      c)   Three   ☐

      d)   It makes no difference   ☐

      e)   No minimum is recommended   ☐

7:    What name is given to an Off-Specification which is accepted by the Project Board
      without corrective action?

      a)   An Exception Report   ☐

      b)   An Exception Memo   ☐

      c)   A Contingency Plan   ☐

      d)   A Concession   ☐

      e)   A Project Issue   ☐

8:    When does a Team Manager report on the status of a Work Package to the
      Project Manager?

      a)   Weekly   ☐

      b)   Daily   ☐

      c)   At the frequency defined in the Work Package   ☐

      d)   Ad-hoc   ☐

9:    What comes first in PRINCE2?

      a)   The Project Brief   ☐

      b)   A Feasibility Study   ☐

      c)   A Scoping/Definition Study   ☐

      d)   The Customer's Acceptance Criteria   ☐

      e)   Customer's Quality Expectations   ☐

      f)   A Project Mandate   ☐

10:    Who is appointed in the first sub-process (Starting Up a Project (SU1))?

     a)   The Project Board Executive Member   ☐

     b)   The Project Manager   ☐

     c)   Both the above   ☐

     d)   The Project Board   ☐

     e)   The Project Management Team   ☐

11:    Which of these processes does NOT trigger the Planning (PL) Process?

     a)   Controlling a Stage (CS)   ☐

     b)   Starting Up a Project (SU)   ☐

     c)   Managing Stage Boundaries (SB)   ☐

     d)   Initiating a Project (IP)   ☐

12:    Which of these is NOT a specific objective of an End Stage Assessment?

     a)   Check that the need for the project is unchanged   ☐

     b)   Review the next Stage Plan against the Project Plan   ☐

     c)   Disseminate useful lessons learned   ☐

     d)   Review the tolerances set for the next stage   ☐

13:    Does PRINCE2 cover …

     a)   The product lifecycle?   ☐

     b)   The project lifecycle?   ☐

     c)   The project lifecycle plus some pre-project preparation?   ☐

     d)   The product lifecycle plus some post-project activity?   ☐

     e)   The complete project and product lifecycle?   ☐

14:    What provision can be made in Planning for implementing requests for dealing with expected change?

     a)   Project and Stage Tolerances   ☐

     b)   A Change Budget   ☐

     c)   Contingency Plans   ☐

     d)   Adding contingency to estimates   ☐

15: In the Planning Process, which sub-process comes before 'Estimating'?

- a) Identifying Activities and Dependencies ☐
- b) Analysing Risks ☐
- c) Completing a Plan ☐
- d) Scheduling ☐
- e) Defining and Analysing Products ☐

16: What action should a Reviewer take on finding a minor (e.g. grammar) mistake in a product under review?

- a) Note it on an Error List ☐
- b) Advise the Producer ☐
- c) Note it on the Follow-up Action List ☐
- d) Annotate the product copy ☐
- e) Advise the Quality Review Scribe ☐

17: Which of these statements is FALSE?

- a) A PRINCE2 project has a finite life span ☐
- b) A PRINCE2 project has a defined amount of resources ☐
- c) A PRINCE2 project has an organisation structure with defined responsibilities to manage the project ☐
- d) A PRINCE2 project may have only activities with no associated products ☐

18: Which of these is NOT a Project Issue?

- a) An Exception Report ☐
- b) A Request for Change ☐
- c) A Specialist Query ☐
- d) A Statement of Concern ☐
- e) All the above ☐

19:    Who is responsible for the 'Managing Product Delivery (MP)' process?

    a)   The Project Manager ☐

    b)   The Senior Supplier ☐

    c)   The Stage Manager ☐

    d)   The Team Manager ☐

20:    Which stage does PRINCE2 suggest should always be used?

    a)   Implementation ☐

    b)   Testing ☐

    c)   Start-up ☐

    d)   Initiation ☐

    e)   Handover ☐

21:    Identify the two possible allowances which may have to be included within the project's plan structure

    a)   A Change Budget and Contingency Plans ☐

    b)   Plan Levels and Planning Tools ☐

    c)   Impact Analysis and Concessions ☐

    d)   Exception Reporting and Exception Assessments ☐

22:    What is created first in Product-based Planning?

    a)   A Product Checklist ☐

    b)   Product Descriptions ☐

    c)   A Product Flow Diagram ☐

    d)   Product Outlines ☐

    e)   A Product Breakdown Structure ☐

23:    'Controlling a Stage (CS)' drives which other process?

    a)   Ad-Hoc Direction ☐

    b)   Planning ☐

    c)   Managing Stage Boundaries ☐

    d)   Managing Product Delivery ☐

    e)   Closing a Project ☐

24:     Which individual role is ultimately responsible for the project?

   a)   Senior User   ☐

   b)   Senior Supplier   ☐

   c)   Executive   ☐

   d)   Project Manager   ☐

   e)   Programme Director   ☐

25:     In which process is the Project Management Team reviewed for changes?

   a)   Planning a Stage   ☐

   b)   Reporting Stage End   ☐

   c)   Updating a Project Plan   ☐

   d)   Reviewing Stage Status   ☐

26:     What is a direct input to the Project Quality Plan?

   a)   ISO9001 QMS   ☐

   b)   The Corporate Quality Policy   ☐

   c)   The Business Case   ☐

   d)   Quality Reviewers' Assignments   ☐

   e)   Customer's Quality Expectations   ☐

27:     Which management product 'drives' the project?

   a)   The Risk Assessment (and Risk Log)   ☐

   b)   The Project Initiation Document   ☐

   c)   The Project Brief   ☐

   d)   The Business Case   ☐

   e)   The Project Mandate   ☐

28:     Project Controls are set up based on the Project Brief, the Project Quality Plan, and …

   a)   The Project Plan   ☐

   b)   The Risk Log   ☐

   c)   The Business Case   ☐

   d)   The Project Approach   ☐

   e)   The Project Mandate   ☐

29:   Name the product which measures the achievement of the project's benefits

  a)   End Project Notification   ☐

  b)   Lessons Learned Report   ☐

  c)   End Project Report   ☐

  d)   Post Project Review   ☐

  e)   Benefits Review Statement   ☐

30:   In which process is the Stage Plan updated with 'actuals'?

  a)   Assessing Progress   ☐

  b)   Reviewing Stage Status   ☐

  c)   Planning a Stage   ☐

  d)   Reporting Highlights   ☐

31:   When do the steps of 'Directing a Project' begin?

  a)   Before 'Starting up a Project'   ☐

  b)   At initiation of the project   ☐

  c)   During 'Starting up a Project'   ☐

  d)   After 'Starting up a Project'   ☐

  e)   From the receipt of the Project Mandate   ☐

32:   What does PRINCE2 regard as the third project interest, given user and supplier as the other two?

  a)   Technical   ☐

  b)   Management   ☐

  c)   Business   ☐

  d)   Quality   ☐

  e)   Sponsor/Customer   ☐

33:   Which of the following is part of 'Accepting a Work Package'?

  a)   Understand the reporting requirements   ☐

  b)   Agree tolerance for the project   ☐

  c)   Monitor and control the risks associated with the Work Package   ☐

  d)   Producing Checkpoint Reports   ☐

34:   Which statement is incorrect? Stages are …

  a)   The amount of work defined in a Work Package ☐

  b)   Partitions of the project with decision points ☐

  c)   Collections of activities and products whose delivery is managed as a unit ☐

  d)   A sub-set of the project ☐

  e)   The element of work which the Project Manager is managing on behalf of the Project Board at any one time ☐

35:   When should Reviewers be appointed for Quality Review?

  a)   At project planning time ☐

  b)   At stage planning time ☐

  c)   At Quality Review planning time ☐

  d)   As early as possible in the project ☐

36:   What time-driven control advises the status of stage or team work?

  a)   Highlight Report ☐

  b)   Checkpoint Report ☐

  c)   End Stage Report ☐

  d)   Exception Report ☐

  e)   Product Review Status Report ☐

  f)   Quality Review Sign-off ☐

37:   Which one of these forms part of a PRINCE2 plan?

  a)   The Project Organisation ☐

  b)   The Issues Log ☐

  c)   Error Lists ☐

  d)   The Risk Log ☐

  e)   Points at which progress will be monitored and controlled ☐

38:   What purpose is Risk Evaluation concerned with?

   a)   Assessing the probability and impact of individual risks   ☐

   b)   Determines how important each risk is   ☐

   c)   Determines potential risks to be faced   ☐

   d)   Assesses the consequences of each risk   ☐

39:   The configuration of the final deliverable of the project is:

   a)   The final product itself   ☐

   b)   The interim products   ☐

   c)   Its Product Description   ☐

   d)   The sum total of its products   ☐

40:   In which process is the Project Brief created?

   a)   Starting up a Project (SU)   ☐

   b)   Initiating a Project (IP)   ☐

   c)   Authorising Initiation (DP1)   ☐

   d)   Authorising a Project (DP2)   ☐

   e)   In the Project Mandate   ☐

41:   Which phrase applies to the user representative(s) in a PRINCE2 Project Management Team?

   a)   They will be impacted by the outcome   ☐

   b)   They may need to use in-house and/or external teams to construct the final outcome   ☐

   c)   They will provide the funding for the project   ☐

   d)   They are responsible for the final outcome   ☐

42:   What other control is closely linked with Configuration Management?

   a)   Control of risk   ☐

   b)   Project Closure   ☐

   c)   Quality Review   ☐

   d)   Project Initiation   ☐

   e)   Change Control   ☐

43:     When are the planned start and end dates added to the Product Checklist?

    a)   Scheduling ☐

    b)   Completing a Plan ☐

    c)   Analysing Risks ☐

    d)   After 'Authorising a Project (DP2)' ☐

    e)   Updating a Project Plan ☐

44:     Who should re-evaluate the priority of a Project Issue after impact analysis?

    a)   The Project Manager ☐

    b)   Those with project assurance responsibilities ☐

    c)   The Senior User ☐

    d)   The Executive Member ☐

    e)   The Author/Originator ☐

45:     What is the input to the process 'Authorising a Project'?

    a)   The Project Brief ☐

    b)   The Project Plan ☐

    c)   A draft Project Initiation Document ☐

    d)   The project's Business Case ☐

46:     In the sub-process 'Updating a Project Plan' which other products are possibly revised?

    a)   The Risk Log and Business Case ☐

    b)   The Project Quality Plan and Project Approach ☐

    c)   The Project Management Team and Project Brief ☐

    d)   The Lessons Learned Report and End Stage Report ☐

    e)   The Project Mandate, Project Brief and PID ☐

47:     What is the correct order of creation given (a) = Product Description,

(b) = Product Breakdown Structure and (c) = Product Flow Diagram?

a)   a, b, c   ☐

b)   b, a, c   ☐

c)   c, a, b   ☐

d)   b, c, a   ☐

e)   a, c, b   ☐

48:     Which of the following is NOT a PRINCE2 definition of a project?

a)   Has a finite and defined life span   ☐

b)   Produces defined and measurable business products   ☐

c)   Uses a defined amount of resources   ☐

d)   Has an organisation structure   ☐

e)   Uses a defined set of techniques   ☐

49:     Which of these is NOT a valid risk management action?

a)   Prevention   ☐

b)   Reduction   ☐

c)   Denial   ☐

d)   Transference   ☐

e)   Acceptance   ☐

50:     Which of the following is NOT included in the composition list of the Project
        Initiation Document Product Outline?

a)   Project Mandate   ☐

b)   Initial Business Case   ☐

c)   Project Quality Plan   ☐

d)   Contingency Plan   ☐

51: In which process are Checkpoint Reports created?

  a) Assessing Progress ☐

  b) Reporting Highlights ☐

  c) Reviewing Stage Status ☐

  d) Executing a Work Package ☐

52: The two major types of file suggested by PRINCE2 are a Management File and …

  a) A Technical File ☐

  b) A Specialist File ☐

  c) A System File ☐

  d) A Products File ☐

53: In which process is an Exception Report created?

  a) Reporting Highlights ☐

  b) Escalating Project Issues ☐

  c) Taking Corrective Action ☐

  d) Reviewing Stage Status ☐

  e) Assessing Progress ☐

54: In which process should the customer's quality expectations first be understood?

  a) Starting up a Project ☐

  b) Initiating a Project ☐

  c) Authorising a Project ☐

  d) Authorising Initiation ☐

55: Risk Evaluation comprises Risk Probability and …

  a) Risk Assessment ☐

  b) Risk Reduction ☐

  c) Risk Impact ☐

  d) Risk Planning ☐

56: Which product lists the major products to be produced, with their key delivery dates?

    a)   Product Breakdown Structure   ☐

    b)   Product Description   ☐

    c)   Product Flow Diagram   ☐

    d)   Product Checklist   ☐

57: Which function creates, maintains and monitors the use of a Quality System?

    a)   Quality Assurance   ☐

    b)   Project Support   ☐

    c)   The Project Assurance Team   ☐

    d)   The Project Board   ☐

58: On completion of a Work Package, assessment of the work performed may contribute to what?

    a)   Highlight Reporting   ☐

    b)   Checkpoint Reporting   ☐

    c)   Performance Appraisal   ☐

    d)   Assessing Progress   ☐

59: Refining the Business Case and Risk Log updates …

    a)   The Project Plan   ☐

    b)   The Issues Log   ☐

    c)   The Project Brief   ☐

60: Risk Impact should ideally be considered under the headings of time, quality, benefits and …

    a)   Estimates   ☐

    b)   Business Case   ☐

    c)   The users   ☐

    d)   People   ☐

61: Quality management is ensuring that …

   a)   A quality management system is created   ☐

   b)   The customer's quality expectations are met   ☐

   c)   Quality requirements are met   ☐

   d)   Product quality criteria are set   ☐

62: What is the name of the job a Team Manager carries out for the Project Manager?

   a)   A Team Plan   ☐

   b)   A Product Description   ☐

   c)   A Work Package   ☐

   d)   Resolving a Project Issue   ☐

63: In which file is the Risk Log kept?

   a)   The Project File   ☐

   b)   The Specialist File   ☐

   c)   The Risks File   ☐

   d)   The Products File   ☐

   e)   The Stage File   ☐

   f)   The Quality File   ☐

64: In the Process 'Decommissioning a Project' the files are archived – what is the reason for this?

   a)   To provide useful lessons learned   ☐

   b)   To permit future audit   ☐

   c)   It is good practice never to throw anything away ☐

   d)   To provide management information   ☐

65: A list of the major products to be produced is a component of …

   a)   Configuration Management   ☐

   b)   A Product Description   ☐

   c)   A Plan   ☐

   d)   The Project Mandate   ☐

66:   What are described as the 'assets' of a project?

    a)   Its business benefits ☐

    b)   Its resources ☐

    c)   The products ☐

    d)   The plans ☐

    e)   The Project Management Team ☐

67:   The Project Plan is based on the Project Brief, the Project Quality Plan and which other product?

    a)   The Project Approach ☐

    b)   The Business Case ☐

    c)   The Issue Log ☐

    d)   The Risk Log ☐

    e)   The Project Initiation Document ☐

68:   Apart from the Issue Log, what else is updated by the Process 'Examining Project Issues'?

    a)   Lessons Learned ☐

    b)   Business Case ☐

    c)   Risk Log ☐

    d)   Stage Plan ☐

69:   Which of these is NOT an input to 'Producing An Exception Plan (SB6)'?

    a)   Current Stage Plan ☐

    b)   Exception Report ☐

    c)   Lessons Learned Report ☐

    d)   Issues Log ☐

70:   In the Business Case component, GAP analysis …

     a)   Takes three views of the achievement of benefits – good, average and poor   ☐

     b)   Measures the difference between success and failure   ☐

     c)   Defines benefits in terms of 'General', 'Anticipated' and 'Probable'   ☐

     d)   Is a required step within Risk Evaluation   ☐

     e)   Is an essential and sensible part of Risk Planning   ☐

71:   Which product is not created within the PRINCE2 process model?

     a)   The Project Plan   ☐

     b)   The Project Mandate   ☐

     c)   The Project Brief   ☐

     d)   The Business Case   ☐

     e)   The Project Initiation Document   ☐

72:   In which top-level process are the files for the project created?

     a)   Starting up a Project   ☐

     b)   Initiating a Project   ☐

     c)   Controlling a Stage   ☐

     d)   Managing Product Delivery   ☐

73:   The four layers of the PRINCE2 Organisation Structure are Corporate or Programme Management, Day-to-Day Management of the Project, Team Management and …

     a)   User Management   ☐

     b)   Supplier Management   ☐

     c)   Customer Direction   ☐

     d)   Direction of the Project   ☐

74: In Sensitivity Analysis the main aim is …

    a)   To determine how important a particular risk is   ☐

    b)   To ensure that no inaccurate statements are included in the Business Case put forward to the Executive   ☐

    c)   To provide a strong, robust Business Case analysis   ☐

    d)   To see if the Business Case is heavily dependent on a particular benefit   ☐

75: Which of the following is NOT a typical Specialist Product?

    a)   The specification of the project's outcome   ☐

    b)   The Risk Log for the project   ☐

    c)   The test results for a major product of the project   ☐

    d)   A colour laser printer required for an IT system project   ☐

Total Score:

Marking your paper

Now you have completed the example Foundation Examination paper, check your answers against those shown in the following table and look up the page number references for any questions you answered incorrectly. You should, ideally, be looking for a score of between 60–65 correct answers and completion within 40–50 minutes. Remember, for the actual examination you need to score 38 correct answers in 60 minutes.

Question	Answer	Question	Answer	Question	Answer
1	C	26	E	51	D
2	E	27	D	52	B
3	B	28	B	53	B
4	A	29	D	54	A
5	A	30	A	55	C
6	B	31	D	56	D
7	D	32	C	57	A
8	C	33	A	58	C
9	F	34	A	59	A
10	C	35	B	60	D
11	A	36	B	61	B
12	C	37	E	62	C
13	C	38	A	63	A
14	B	39	D	64	B
15	A	40	A	65	C
16	D	41	A	66	C
17	D	42	E	67	A
18	A	43	B	68	C
19	D	44	C	69	C
20	D	45	C	70	A
21	A	46	B	71	B
22	E	47	B	72	B
23	D	48	E	73	D
24	C	49	C	74	D
25	A	50	A	75	B

The Practitioner Examination

You must first have passed the PRINCE2 Foundation Examination in order to sit the Practitioner Examination. The Practitioner Examination is a three-hour, open-book examination. You may take the PRINCE2 manual and any notes (including this book) into the examination. A computer or any other electronic reference material is not allowed. The examination is designed to test your ability to apply the principles of the method to a given scenario, by answering specific questions. There are three questions and a short scenario similar to the following.

Questions

Q1 How would you advise your colleague to tackle her organisation's quality expectations using the approaches in PRINCE2?

Q2 Demonstrate your understanding of the scope of the project by producing a Product Breakdown Structure and Product Flow Diagram for the Specialist Products of the project

Q3 Explain how the PRINCE2 concept of stages will help to control the project. Draw a diagram showing how and where the stages might occur on your colleague's project

Scenario

You have a colleague who is an experienced manager and administrator, but she is new to project management.

She has been assigned to manage the creation, publication and initial distribution of the company's next annual mail order catalogue. The catalogue is aimed at the top end of a traditionally very demanding market and her management is concerned about building in quality as last year's publication went out late and with a number of errors.

The catalogue will, as before, contain text and photographs printed on premium glossy paper. A photographic studio will be employed to provide up to 500 finished photographs of the company's products.

It is intended to place a contract for creation of the text (describing the photographed products) with a professional copy-writing company. In the past, supporting text has been produced internally but there is a feeling that past efforts have been rather amateurish and lacking in 'customer appeal'. The decision to out-source this major and vital part of the catalogue has come directly from the Managing Director and she has a lot riding on the outcome. The copy-writing company has just won a similar contract from a major competitor of your colleague's company and there is some disquiet about security and where loyalties might lie.

The company has no printing capability and will, as in the past, arrange for printing and distribution to be handled by outside, independent, companies. The printing company has offered to arrange distribution through a sub-contractor, and has also offered to co-ordinate all catalogue production aspects as they have good, long-term, relationships with the photographic studio and copy-writing company, as well as other sources in these fields. No decision has yet been made on this proposal.

Organisation

Your colleague normally reports to a senior manager who in turn reports to a Board-level Director. For this project, she has been told she will report directly to the Managing Director.

There are about four months available for this project to be brought to completion and your colleague is obviously anxious to deliver a suitable end-product but is worried about the amount of work she will be expected to do herself, as she has no specialist experience of the printing world.

A lot is riding on this project for all levels of management within the company. The market is very competitive and customers can be lost easily to some vigorous newcomers.

The examiner's preferred answer style is the use of 'bullet' points, followed by up to three sentences (no more!) to show the examiner that you understand the **purpose**, **when it happens**, **who does it** and, where appropriate, the **content**; do not hide these vital, mark-scoring, points within an essay!

The marks available for each answer are divided between relatively few marks for the correct **identification** of an expected topic, plus an additional set of bonus marks for correctly **answering** the specific question, **explaining** the topic, **referring** to the PRINCE2 method, and **relating** it to the scenario in the question paper. All answers must use the **correct PRINCE2 terminology** – generic responses will not attract sufficient marks to pass the Practitioner Examination.

A simplified example of how marks are distributed between relevant topics is shown in the table, which illustrates how the examiner's marking scheme is structured and the way in which marks are allocated. The examiner will apportion marks generally on a one-third/two-thirds basis as indicated on the chart below. About one-third of the marks will be awarded for correctly identifying the relevant PRINCE2 topics, and around two-thirds of the available marks will be awarded for describing the relevance and usage of the topic as related to the specific question in the context of the given scenario.

Basically what is needed is to reference the appropriate PRINCE2 element, and then explain and relate its nature, relevance and importance to the question posed; perhaps the two most important things to remember are to explain why you are making a particular recommendation and to relate it to the scenario.

TOPIC (Looked for by the examiner)	Identify	Explain and Relate
Quality Expectations in Project Brief (+ Project Mandate)	1	–
Planning Quality, Quality Plan (IP1); Responsibilities; QMS	1	3
Work Package Authorisation + Agreement Project Manager/Team Manager	2	2
Product Descriptions; Quality Criteria	2	3

A checklist

The following checklist will help you to focus on the appropriate approach to the Practitioner Examination paper. Use it to guide you in preparing for and answering the questions in the paper.

● Start your answer with bullet points, listing the names of those elements of PRINCE2 that address the problem defined in the question

● The only preamble should be one sentence which states, for example: 'The PRINCE2 elements which address this problem are …'. Do not waste time 'setting the scene' or reminding the examiner what the question was

● Expand on each bullet point with no more than three sentences which demonstrate that you understand:

  ■ what it is

  ■ when it is introduced into the project lifecycle

  ■ the purpose it serves

  ■ how it works.

● Don't refer the examiner to the PRINCE2 manual for a 'fuller explanation'

● Don't make assumptions about the examiner's knowledge of the PRINCE2 element you are describing!

● By all means explain (in one sentence) any assumptions you are making about the scenario but beware of wasting time as you will not gain any marks from this

● Don't make any assumptions about the prior use of any part of PRINCE2 in the project scenario unless these are specifically stated

● Don't waffle – if a sentence will not make a specific point about a PRINCE2 element which contributes to the answer, don't write it

● Answer the question – no marks are awarded for mentioning a PRINCE2 element which does not apply to that question. For example, if the question is about quality, don't mention that the Project Board review the Business Case at each End Stage Assessment (ESA); do mention that the ESA provides an opportunity to confirm quality via the Project Assurance roles

● You get more marks for relating your answer to the scenario than for copying the generic point straight from the PRINCE2 manual; the aim is to show how the point would be applied to the specific scenario situation. Do not copy sections from the PRINCE2 reference manual – the examiners will not award any marks for this.

The problems

Since the introduction of the original PRINCE2 Professional Examinations in January 1997, most of the failures (about 35%) have stemmed from the Practitioner Examination. The reasons are varied, with some candidates simply running out of time and failing to score sufficient marks for the final question. Most failed because they either failed to answer the question posed (and produced an answer that was easier to write but irrelevant!) or were unable to make the all-important connections between the scenario, the question, their experience and the PRINCE2 method.

There is usually little doubt that candidates understand the method, proven by the relatively low failure rate in the Foundation Examination (less than 5%) which tests *knowledge* of PRINCE2, and most are sensible middle-managers with at least some practical experience of project management. So the conclusion is that the problems lie with:

- time management
- information retrieval
- examination technique.

Reading time

Under current APM Group rules, candidates for the Practitioner Examination are allowed 10 minutes reading time. During this period you are not allowed to look up or write anything. You will be allowed to highlight, and to make notes on, the examination question paper. You will *not* be allowed to refer to the PRINCE2 reference manual, make notes on anything other than the question paper, leave the room or to discuss the paper with the invigilator or other candidates.

Use the reading time carefully. Highlight the relevant points the scenario is making. You should aim to understand fully the background and the questions by the time the examination starts.

When reading the questions, underline the verbs to ensure you understand what the question is asking you to do. For example you might be asked to **create** a particular plan or diagram; or the question might ask you to **explain** or **describe** a particular element of PRINCE2. Many candidates who fail the Practitioner Examination do so because they have not answered the question posed.

Time management

The requirement for passing the Practitioner Examination is that you must score at least 50% of the marks available. With 50 marks available for each of the three questions, a total of 75 marks must be gained to achieve a pass. The marks are averaged over all the questions so it is possible (but difficult) to compensate for a poorly answered question elsewhere in the paper.

The main problem is that an early answer scoring low marks cannot possibly be compensated for in the final question if you run out of time and are unable to complete the final question. This seems an obvious statement but is a common occurrence!

The remedy is to ensure that the best use is made of the time available; a reasonable approach is to aim for 'a mark per minute' allowing about 50 minutes to be allocated to each question. This should enable you sufficient time to score around 30–40 marks per question, which is about as many as you can reasonably expect under examination conditions. Most questions (but not all) will indicate a breakdown of the marks available for each part, so allocation of writing time to each part of the question, based on a 'mark per minute' will not be difficult.

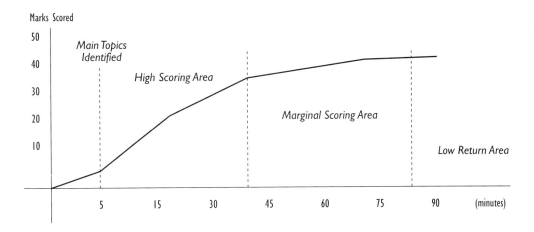

But you must be disciplined!

Most marks will be scored during the first part of the answer – typically the content written after the first five minutes and before the end of 45 minutes. On this basis you should start a new question after writing for no longer than 50 minutes.

Always begin a new question on a separate sheet and number each answer sheet individually: Question 1, Sheet 1, etc. This will enable you to return to your answer and add additional content during the final 10–15 minutes of the examination. Although it might seem to be potentially confusing and time-wasting having to pick up momentum again on each question, the PRINCE2 method is so inherently integrated that you are almost bound to recall additional key points as you tackle the other questions. Don't expect to pick up too many additional marks but even one or two extra marks might help and you might just identify something significant that you failed to cover during the first pass.

Always leave time to read through your work. This will disclose missing references and possibly missing key points. Allow about 15 minutes for this – if you find any major omissions and don't have time to write up the full text, just bullet-point the key features and you will be given marks for including them.

Information retrieval

A problem often encountered when preparing for the examination is the identification of the key points that form the structure of the answer. The options open are to:

- simply 'brain-dump' all the related topics onto a sheet

- go through the contents list of the PRINCE2 manual and identify all relevant topics

- select the appropriate components, processes or techniques referred to in the question and extract the information directly from the appropriate chapters in the PRINCE2 manual

- do something more speedy and productive than any of the above!

The brain-dump approach

This technique assumes that you have sufficient knowledge of the subject matter and the ability to retrieve the most important parts. Some people have this ability and find the technique fast and accurate enough to pass the examination – unfortunately most don't!

Brain-dumping is by its nature unstructured and 'hit and miss' for most of us; lots of fairly irrelevant points, reflecting our own feelings and experiences, always surface and they invariably take a lot of time to write down and sort into some sort of logical order and priority. Unless you are well practised, avoid this approach.

The contents list approach

The PRINCE2 manual contents list addresses the whole of the method and is an excellent full reference. Unfortunately its very comprehensiveness works against it as a technique for preparing for the examination as the time taken to work through the eight A4 sides of contents is time-consuming and unexciting.

To use this technique, ensure that you have a clear view of what you are seeking – essentially a 'scope' – otherwise you might just end up rewriting the whole contents each time you address a question! Write the main topic being interrogated at the top of your answer paper and list the bullet points (and possibly page references) underneath. You will need to be very focused to ensure that only relevant points are identified; aim for 12–15 topic points.

Referring to the PRINCE2 manual contents list is a useful way to check your list of topics produced by other methods. A quick scan can deliver additional relevant points and help your confidence levels.

Using the PRINCE2 manual to identify the topics

This is the most time-consuming approach and has inherent dangers, the chief being that it is all too easy to become focused on just one topic area and ignore the all-important scenario spin-offs that will earn the marks you need to pass the examination.

The examiner is looking for a demonstration that you understand the elements of the PRINCE2 method and are able to apply it to the given scenario, at the same time addressing the question. It is all too easy to become bogged down in the detail of a particular topic and omit reference to other associated elements.

For example, if the question asks how PRINCE2 quality aspects can contribute to a scenario where the customer has concerns about quality, the answer must address not only the rather obvious 'Quality in a Project Environment' component, but also who has responsibility – the 'Organisation' component and the role descriptions in Appendix B of the PRINCE2 manual. You should also discuss the means of achieving quality ('Work Packages' in the 'Controlling A Stage' and 'Managing Product Delivery' processes). Obviously the 'Quality Review' technique and the connections with 'Product Descriptions' and their 'Quality Criteria' must also be established, described and discussed in the context of the set scenario.

To identify all these major topic areas (and many others not mentioned) would take a considerable time going through the PRINCE2 manual; certainly more time than is available in the three-hour examination! You might best be advised to keep the PRINCE2 reference manual closed for most of the time and use it mainly to look up references.

The key topics must be identified, however, and pre-examination preparation to pull out the relevant key topic areas will help on the day. Remember you are allowed to take into the examination any notes you make during your preparation, as well as any training event notes and documentation you possess – so time taken in advance will be well spent.

An alternative approach

If you have followed the guidance in this booklet during your preparation for the Foundation Examination, you will have prepared both a high-level and in-depth 'Process Diagram' showing all the processes and sub-processes, and the related flows of management products.

You can use your high-level Process Diagram to follow the normal route of a project picking up the PRINCE2 topic headings for which you are searching. Each time you identify a relationship between a PRINCE2 process flow you should note down the topic heading that will be used as the basis for writing your answer. You should aim for about 12–15 main topic areas, which when integrated and combined will give you six to eight key paragraph headings. Spend no more than five minutes on this exercise, especially if using it during the PRINCE2 Examination. Using the example question paper, the following customer quality concerns topics might well be identified using this approach:

- Customer's Quality Expectations
- Organisation – Project Board; Senior User
    - User/Customer Involvement
- Organisation – Project Assurance; Senior User
- Planning for Quality – the Quality Path
- Configuration Management
    - Quality Log
- Work Packages; Project Manager and Team Manager Agreement
    - Quality Reviews and QR Technique
    - Product Descriptions
    - Quality Criteria
- Feedback
    - Highlight Reports
    - Checkpoint Reports
    - End Stage Assessments

Once the main topic areas have been identified, the answer can be written up by reference to bullet-point headings supported by short explanations; remember the examiner will be trying to spot the main answer scheme topics and then judge the extent to which you have provided a full answer with reference to the question and scenario.

All questions stand alone. If a point comes up which you have already made in answer to an earlier question, make it again – do not refer back to the answer to a previous question.

Structuring your answer

The marking scheme used by the examiner has already been described. Being able to retrieve all the relevant information will not necessarily result in a successful paper. This is because about two-thirds of the marks awarded relate to the candidate's ability to apply the PRINCE2 elements identified to the particular scenario. To maximise your mark collecting, your answer to each of the three questions should aim to reflect this marking approach. Consider the following strategy:

- Use the checklist suggested for the example question on quality, grouping together related topics to produce 6–8 main paragraph headings
- Plan to split each answer into two – one-third explaining the PRINCE2 elements that apply and two-thirds relating those elements to the scenario.

You have two basic options when actually writing your answer – the diagram and text illustrate this.

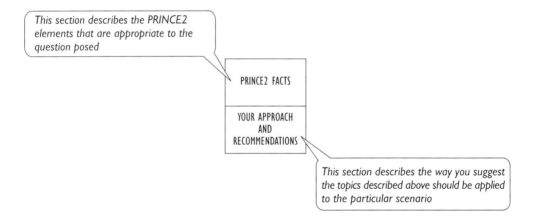

This is the simplest way to produce your answer – it enables a clear separation between factual information available from the PRINCE2 manual and your thoughts about applying those elements to the question and the scenario.

Its main disadvantage is that each identified element has to be visited twice – once to explain the PRINCE2 point and again to show how you would apply that point to the particular scenario. The benefit of this approach lies mainly in its lack of structural complexity which may well prove a boon under anxious examination conditions!

An example is shown below – the answer is not a complete answer to a full question but an extract taken to illustrate the planning, writing approach and style.

Example scenario

A database migration project with a very tight timescale and management concerns that delays will lead to significant loss of business.

Question

Explain how PRINCE2 may be used to identify and manage the risk

The topics identified are:

- Risk Log – creation, use, update

- Risk Process – identification, evaluation, responses, management

- Risk Evaluation – probability and impact

- Risk Responses – prevention, reduction, transfer, acceptance, contingency

- Risk Management – planning, resourcing, monitoring, reporting

- Risk Ownership

- Risk Tolerance

- Stage Boundaries – minimum update – ESA

- Communication – Checkpoint, Highlight Reports

Risk is defined as 'an uncertainty of outcome'. The following PRINCE2 elements apply to this question.

Risk Log

PRINCE2 requires that the component 'Management of Risk' be applied to every project. Risks are first identified in the 'Starting up a Project' Process (SU4) where the Project Brief is produced and the initial Risk Log is created to capture these initial risks. The Risk Log is used to capture and track the progress of risks as the project proceeds. The initial Risk Log is refined in 'Initiating a Project Process' (IP3: *Refining The Business Case and Risks*) where, typically, a full risk analysis will be carried out, and updated. The Risk Log is revisited in the 'Managing Stage Boundaries' process where the preparatory work for the End Stage Assessment (ESA) is carried out.

Analysis of risk

There are four steps recommended by PRINCE2 to analyse the risks:

- **Risk Identification** – identifying and capturing the potential risks

- **Risk Probability** – measuring the likelihood of each identified risk actually happening

- **Risk Impact** – evaluating the effect of a risk should it happen under the general headings time, quality, benefit and people

- **Risk Responses** – identifying the action(s) to be taken to manage the risk.

Management of risk responses

Once actions to counter the identified and evaluated risks have been decided the risk responses must be managed. This is achieved by **planning** and **resourcing** the risk responses. The plan must then be **monitored** and status **reported** to ensure that early warning is assured and that action is taken to put the countermeasures into effect.

This marks the end of the 'PRINCE2 Topics' section of the answer and the start of the 'Application to the Scenario' section of the answer.

Risk Log

I recommend that a Project Brief be produced and a Risk Log be established. To achieve this I recommend a short meeting between the Project Manager, the Senior User (or User Assurance nominee) the supplier representative and the Executive (or Business Assurance nominee) where an initial risk analysis (i.e. risk identification, evaluation and responses) will indicate the immediate and obvious risks facing the project. To record this I recommend that a Risk Log be created and that it be updated when the risk analysis is refined during the creation of the draft Project Initiation Document. Subsequently I recommend that the risk analysis and the Risk Log be updated, minimally, at the end of each Management Stage in preparation for the Project Board's End Stage Assessment. In addition to this I recommend that the risk analysis be reviewed on a weekly basis for the first month, and the Risk Log updated, because of the management concerns about schedule delay coupled with the substantial negative impact a schedule delay would cause.

Analysis of risks

All the recommended steps of risk analysis/management must be carried out. Under Risk Identification it is likely that schedule delay and loss of existing and new business will be major risks identified. Risk Evaluation must be properly measured in this case as the impact on the company is likely to be substantial; I recommend that the specialist supplier and business resources be involved at a formal risk analysis workshop to ensure all the relevant information is available. I recommend that the evaluation, response, and ownership of each identified risk be considered by the Project Board prior to any commercial decision being taken. Each Project Board member must have the opportunity to input to Risk Evaluation and their attendance at a formal meeting, towards the end of the Risk Workshop, is recommended. To help their deliberations I recommend that proper metrics be used for risk analysis and a 'threshold' figure for an 'unacceptable level of risk' be established and agreed.

Risk responses

Clear decisions about what is and is not an acceptable risk and its owner must be followed up by a statement of the Project Manager's recommendations and by confirmation of Project Board support. I recommend that the Project Board's decisions be recorded and that a physical sign-off is obtained. In this scenario, the high level of business risk makes it unlikely that any major risks would be 'accepted' without some action being proposed. A more proactive approach is necessary with transference and/or sharing of risks with the new supplier being particularly attractive; in any event contingency planning must be put into place.

Management of risks

A properly resourced plan, signed up to by the Project Board (and published to all the Project Management Team) must be prepared as soon as possible after risk responses have been agreed. The risks must be monitored at least every week and the Risk Log and risk plan updated. Any change in circumstance (schedule or resource) must be picked up and reported to the Project Board. A tolerance on risk should be introduced to provide a 'trigger' for when such reference should occur.

Notice how the answer focuses specifically on PRINCE2 for the first part and that, having covered all the major topics, then expands on the answer by applying the identified PRINCE2 elements to the scenario and question. Note also that the answer, as far as it goes, reflects the suggested one-third/two-thirds rule.

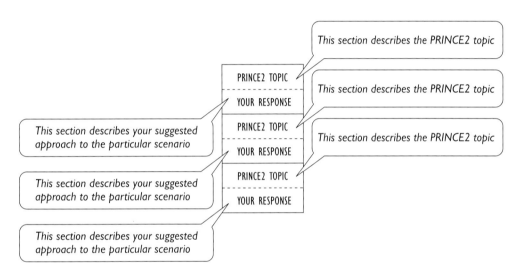

A more refined answer, requiring only one visit to each of the topics, is summarised by the diagram. Each identified topic is described in respect of its PRINCE2 aspect, followed by recommendations on usage within the specific scenario. An example portion of answer for the same scenario and question, using the same text is illustrated below.

Risk is defined as 'an uncertainty of outcome'. The following PRINCE2 elements apply to this question.

Risk Log

PRINCE2 requires that the Component 'Management of Risk' be applied to every project. Risks are first identified in the 'Starting up a Project' Process (SU4) where the Project Brief is created and a Risk Log is created to capture these initial risks.

I recommend that a Project Brief be produced and an initial Risk Log be established. To achieve this I recommend a short meeting between the Project Manager, the Senior User (or User Assurance nominee), the supplier representative and the Executive (or Business Assurance nominee) where an initial risk analysis (i.e. risk identification, evaluation and responses) will point out the immediate and obvious risks facing the project. To record this I recommend that a Risk Log be created and that it be updated when the risk analysis is refined during the creation of the draft Project Initiation Document.

The Risk Log is used to capture and track the progress of risks as the project proceeds. The initial Risk Log is refined in 'Initiating A Project' Process (IP3: *Refining the Business Case and Risks*) where a full risk analysis will be carried out, and updated when the risk analysis is revisited in the 'Managing Stage Boundaries' process, where the preparatory work for the End Stage Assessment (ESA) is carried out.

I recommend that the risk analysis and the Risk Log be updated at the end of each Management Stage in preparation for the Project Board's End Stage Assessment. In addition to this I recommend that the risk analysis be reviewed on a weekly basis for the first month, and the Risk Log updated, because of the management's concerns about schedule delay coupled with the substantial negative impact a schedule delay would cause.

How not to answer a question!

So far this book has discussed the positive aspects of preparing for the examination and has advised on identifying the main topics to be addressed.

The next few pages provide specimen answers to a Practitioner Examination paper which has seen extensive service but which now has been withdrawn. The answers have been written under examination conditions. The examiner's answer scheme is reproduced in the Appendix.

There is, however, some benefit in providing an example of how *not* to write an answer! The following example is taken from a candidate's paper and illustrates an answer that scored very few marks – you are advised to read it and then completely erase it from your memory!

Question

How would you use (if at all) the 'Controlling A Stage (CS)' and 'Managing Product Delivery (MP)' processes in a small project?

The Controlled Stage approach which PRINCE2 adopts would be relevant for a small project, i.e. Controlled Start, Controlled Progress and Controlled Close as this would:

- ensure that the viability of the project was continually being assessed

- ensure that the End Stage Assessments were carried out to enable important decisions to be made before more detailed work was done

- clarify the impact of external events.

In a small project the Initiation Stage and Start Up could be combined as a Controlled Start. The Project Initiation Stage is comparatively short and inexpensive but is essential in order to:

- define the project objectives and how they will be met

- clearly understand and state the Business Case

- identify who the customer is

- outline responsibilities and authority

- determine project boundaries

- document any assumptions that have been made

- identify any risks which may prevent the project achieving a successful outcome

- determine when the major products will be delivered

- determine costs

- determine controls

- determine the stages of the project

- determine Quality Assurance.

At the end of the Project Initiation Stage, the Project Initiation Document would be produced, covering all these questions and this would then become the reference document to show the original basis for the project.

As the end of a stage is a major control point for the Project Board, having gone through the Initiation Stage they would have been in a position to decide whether to continue with the project before incurring any more costs.

The answer to the question is reproduced exactly as presented to the examiner. A simple analysis of content reveals lack of reference to PRINCE2, incorrect terminology and no explanation for each element of **what it is**, **when it is introduced into the project life-cycle**, **the purpose it serves** and **how it works**. The original question was set within a scenario; the answer provides no linkage or cross-reference to the scenario; taken in isolation, there is no way of assessing what the original scenario might have been.

Specimen answers

Specimen answers have been prepared for the three questions posed in the following example paper, and which are reproduced in this chapter. The original answers were all produced under examination conditions. The answer paper has been reviewed by the APMG's Chief Examiner and comments added.

The Practitioner Examination: Scenario 26 v12

Questions

Q1(a) Demonstrate your understanding of the scope of the project by drawing a Product Breakdown Structure for the specialist products for the Project Plan (18 marks)

Q1(b) Create a Product Flow Diagram from the Product Breakdown Structure (18 marks)

Note: The examiner will award up to 14 extra marks for these diagrams where they show a good understanding of the product-planning technique by showing realistic products, based on the scenario, in their diagrams. No extra writing or additional diagrams are required.

Q2(a) Select three risks associated with the scenario and using the PRINCE2 approach carry out a risk analysis giving reasons for each step for each risk (23 marks)

Q2(b) Make proposals for the management of each risk (10 marks)

Q2(c) Identify the major events at which the Project Manager will examine risks (17 marks)

Q3(a) Draw an organisation structure for the project, naming the people who would fill each role (22 marks)

Q3(b) Explain briefly any other project organisation options that you might consider (14 marks)

Q3(c) Suggest suitable stages for the project and give reasons for your choice (14 marks)

Scenario

An American yachting enthusiast has just bought a successful British boatyard on the south coast. The firm has a long order book for the luxury catamarans that it builds. Six vessels are in build, contracts signed, and stage money received. The previous owner has arranged to sell the site currently used by the boatyard. The new owner has leased a hangar on a former airfield, six miles inland, and all the workforce (a foreman, five ship builders and four office staff) are willing to move to the new site. The foreman has inspected the hangar and believes that it is perfectly adequate for the work.

You are a professional, independent Project Manager. You have been asked by the new owner to manage the whole project to set up the new premises and move the company to the new site.

The boatyard machinery has to be dismantled, moved and reassembled at the new site by the boatyard ship builders. A more powerful electricity supply needs to be installed by the local electricity company to supply electricity to the new site to cope with the demands of the machinery.

At present access to the new site is restricted to light traffic because of major roadworks. The local council expects to finish the work by 10 December, and the new road will make it easy to move heavy loads to and from the site.

An office is to be constructed inside the hangar. The ship builders have offered to build this. The foreman has estimated that it would need five ship builders to build the office after he has designed it. Sub-contractors would then install cabling to provide electricity from the new supply to the office and then decorate the office before the office move could take place.

You are tasked to prepare plans for the move to commence on 1 December and be completed by 11 January. The move has to be completed in six weeks because the new owners of the boatyard site intend to start building work on a marina then. They are adamant that there will be no site access for your client after the six weeks.

Your project is responsible for transportation of the six catamarans to the new site. A firm has been approached to carry out the move of the vessels, and has estimated that each yacht move would require two days. The contract firm has only one crane and one yacht transporter suitable for the work. Your project must get a contract signed with the local firm for this work.

Answer script

Question 1(a): Product Breakdown Structure

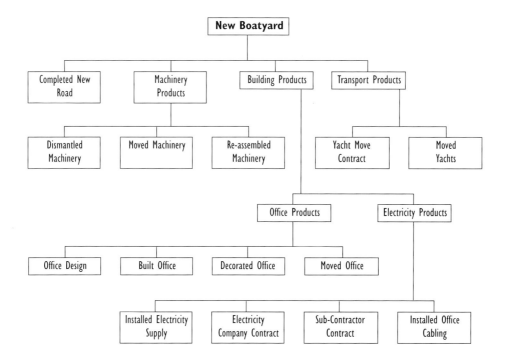

Marker's comments

This is excellent. Good breakdown, sensible products. Captured all the products mentioned in the scenario. All the breakdowns are clearly 'this consists of', with no examples of falling into the trap of breakdowns that mean 'this is followed by'. The only question is whether or not the scenario stated that contracts would be needed for the improved power supply and the later sub-contractor. No matter, although the scenario didn't say this, these are two sensible products and would be added to the candidate's count of products identified. Full marks.

Question 1(b): Product Flow Diagram

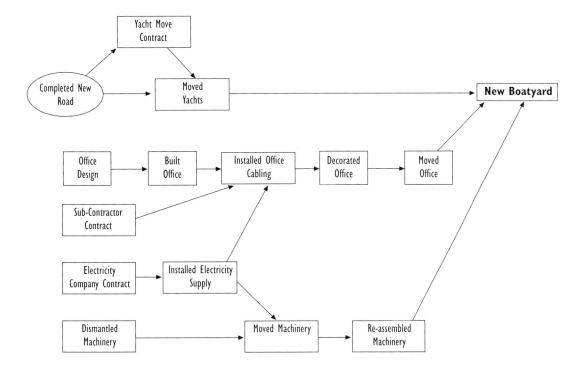

Marker's comments

A good PFD with only a couple of errors. The completed new road is also a dependency of 'moved machinery', and the yacht move contract is not dependent on the completed new road. Otherwise good. The external is correctly identified. The 'installed electricity supply' could have been another external if it had to be done anyway, rather than as a result of a contract within the project's bounds. The arrows are clear, almost made unnecessary by the good left–right flow. Good point was the use of 'new boatyard' as the top of the PBS and the final product in the PFD. The answer gets full marks for accurate match between PBS and PFD names and no use of activities. Only lowest-level products in the PBS have been transferred to the PFD, making it very easy to ensure that all correct products move between the two diagrams. The external product was also correctly listed in the Product Breakdown Structure as well as shown in the PFD.

Question 2(a)

Risk can be defined as uncertainty of outcome. All projects face risks and the project must determine the level of risk it is prepared to tolerate.

This project has many risks inherent due to the short timescale and dependencies on external factors. They fall into the risks categories of strategic/commercial and technical/operational/infrastructure in the main.

Marker's comments

The two paragraphs above say sensible things, but nothing that would gain them marks in the examination. They are too general. Remember, the question simply says 'select three risks'.

Three risks in this project are:

1   delay to commencement of transportation of machinery and vessels due to roadworks not finishing until 10 December

2   delay to vessels transportation due to the contract firm having only one crane and yacht-transporter – legal/regulatory (contracted arrangements)

3   vessels in build not being completed on time due to boatyard move, e.g. machinery does not work when assembled – technical/operational/ infrastructure (increased dismantling time).

Marker's comments

Three clear risks. You could say that the first risk is of the roadworks not finishing until 10 December, which would have the effect of delaying commencement of machinery and vessel transportation; similarly with the other two risks, but the markers would accept these.

The risk log shown is based on the product description outline in PRINCE2. The scores are 1 – low, 2 – medium, and 3 – high. The tolerance score is the probability and impact multiplied together to evaluate the level of risk. Any risk scoring 6 or above would be above the risk tolerance line and not acceptable. These require risk actions to be identified and costed. Any contingency actions should have a contingency budget allocated for use should they occur.

Marker's comments

The table is a useful shorthand way of expressing a lot of information – and reminding the candidate of required entries. Very often candidates give all details for the first risk, but forget one or two entries by the time they are doing the third risk. The table would have been lacking without the following explanation of what the possible range of scoring was and what the tolerance score meant. Remember the manual only uses the high, medium and low categories, so use of anything else should be explained.

Reasons

Risk 1

Road projects are frequently delayed, but tighter contracts are reducing this and so the probability is 2. The impact is 2 because there are four weeks between completion of the road and project completion – only 12 days are needed to move the yachts.

The Executive is the owner as this is a risk from outside the project.

RISK	Category	Impact	Probability	Tolerance Score (Impact × Probability)	Proximity	Risk Response	Response Type	Owner
Transportation delay due to roadwork completion delay	Strategic/ commercial (suppliers)	2	2	4	Close	1. Maintain close links with council regarding finish dates 2. Negotiate extended site access from new owners if risk occurs 3. Plan transportation to commence after road due to be completed	Reduction Contingency Reduction	Executive (New Owner)
Transportation delay due to firm having only one crane and one transporter	Strategic/ commercial (contractual commitment)	3	2	6	Medium	1. Plan for minimum of 3 vessels moved by Xmas give float time 2. Plan for transportation during weekends and bank holidays if needed due to delays 3. Contract penalties for delay 4. Identify alternative if needed	Reduction Contingency Transference Prevention	Project Manager
Vessels in build not completed on time due to project problems. Risk to business e.g. machinery does not work when reassembled	Technical/ operational/ infrastructure (inadequacy of business continuity)	3	1	3	Later	1. Identify plans to catch up from any delays after move or be ahead prior to move 2. Identify priority order for building of yachts 3. Discuss any acceptable delays with purchasers and keep informed of plans	Contingency Reduction Acceptance	Senior User (Foreman)

Risk 2

The probability of the crane or transporters breaking down and delaying the project is medium as the firm is undertaking this work regularly and relies on their machinery for their business viability. The impact would be high as there will be no site access after the six weeks.

The Project Manager is the owner, as he/she is best placed to monitor the risk.

Risk 3

The probability of this happening is low as the move has been planned and it is likely to have been discussed with purchasers. If it happened it would have a high impact as there are considerable costs incurred to the business due to loss of reputation and loss of income. This is why the Senior User has been identified as the owner. I have suggested this would be the foreman as he would have the specialist knowledge to represent all the aspects of the project and would also be impacted by the outcome.

Marker's comments

Three very clear reasons for the estimation of the risks. A common fault made by many candidates is to forget to give reasons, just the table of values. Again the table layout avoided another common fault: failure to mention that PRINCE2 requires each risk to have an owner. The examiner will always expect a sensible suggestion as to who the owner should be – derived from the scenario. The only thing missing from the answer is risk evaluation; the balance of the cost of the risk occurring against the cost of the possible risk actions.

Question 2(b)

Risks need to be managed and the first step in this is to identify them and log them.

The three risks identified then need planning, resourcing, monitoring, reporting and budgeting.

The risks would be logged as soon as identified, not as part of risk management.

Risk 1

Responses for countermeasures would be:

1   maintain close links with council

2   negotiate extended site access

3   plan transportation later than road completion.

Resourcing will need time of the Executive for 1, Project management for 2 and 3, so costed for by time.

Risk 2

Responses would be:

1   plan minimum three vessels moved by Xmas

2   contingency to use weekends and bank holidays if delays incurred

3   contract penalties for delays

4   identify alternative method, e.g. airlift between sites.

Resourcing will need time of Project Manager for 1, 2, 3 and 4 and costs of this time. Additional contingency costs are needed for 4.

Risk 3

Responses would be:

1   plan to catch up from any delays and/or be ahead prior to moves

2   identify buildings order by date urgency/priority

3   discuss acceptability of delays with purchasers and keep informed of plans.

Resourcing will require time of foreman for 1 and 2, with 3 being carried out by either the Executive or someone delegated by them. Again costs associated with this time need to be planned.

Marker's comments

A choice of risk responses is part of risk analysis, not risk management. Marks can, at the examiner's discretion, be awarded for comments made in a different section of the same question. In this case, these comments would be added to those in the table in the answer to Q1(a). Marks cannot, however, cross question boundaries, e.g. a point made in answer to Q2 cannot earn marks in Q1. The resourcing comments made at the end of each set of actions show who would be needed to take action, plus the costs. The comments seem intended to cover the first two steps of risk management – planning and resourcing.

All three risks need to be monitored and reported on. I recommend that a risk profile is used and shown in Highlight Reports to Project Board. Checkpoint Reports from the teams will be frequent and have risk status identified. The Project Manager will review risks frequently with some daily when the proximity is close.

As a minimum they are updated at each stage end but this is a high-risk project and the Project Manager will monitor them more frequently.

Marker's comments

The answer made two points about reporting: Checkpoint Report, Highlight Report; and two about monitoring: End Stage Assessment and daily reports. The answer will thus get some marks for this part, but it would have been clearer to mention that Highlight Reports are from the Project Manager, the Project Manager using the Daily Log to record moments at which to monitor risks and then record any status change in the Risk Log. The Project Manager reports on risk status in the End Stage Report, which will allow the Project Board to monitor risks as part of their End Stage Assessment.

Question 2(c)

The Project Manager needs to keep a close eye on the risks in this project to ensure all vessels and machinery are moved while access is available to the new site.

Marker's comments

This is correct, but a general comment that would not earn marks. Remember, if a sentence doesn't make a specific PRINCE2 point, don't write it.

Risks are at first identified when preparing the Project Brief and the Risk Log is established. The Risk Log will then be updated in IP3 when refining the Business Case and risks. Further risks come to light and more information is available for risks already identified as more detail is gathered about the project. The planning process requires risks to be analysed prior to completion of any plan. The Project Quality Plan (PQP) and Project Plan have been developed and so new risks will have been identified.

Marker's comments

The answer is a mixture of process identifiers (IP3) and process descriptions (preparing the Project Brief). Both are acceptable and earn marks.

The Project Manager will continually assess information from checkpoints CS2 and add information to the Risk Log where appropriate. They also capture and examine Project Issues, CS3 and 4, which are likely to identify some further risks.

Marker's comments

CS3 does not update the Risk Log, but marks would be earned for CS2 and CS4.

This project is likely to have many Project Issues arise due to reliance on third parties (electricity and transportation) and interdependence on another project (road).

At each point that stage status is reviewed (CS5) the Risk Log is reviewed to ensure that it is up to date and there are no risks to completion of the current stage. When preparing for ESAs the risks are updated by the Project Manager in SB4 to go to the Project Board.

Time is critical in this project and tight tolerance is likely to be in place. This is appropriate as there are high risks associated with time. The Project Manager will examine the risk – particularly those associated with time – prior to every Highlight Report to the Project Board (CS6). Any changes in status or new ones will be in the report.

Marker's comments

There were marks available for identifying that time was critical and that there should be a tight time tolerance connected to keeping a close eye on the risk associated with any time slippage.

Question 3(a): Organisation Structure

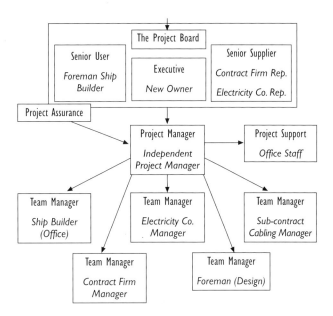

Reasons

User – The foreman will be impacted by the outcome as will the ship builder. There are two Senior Users because there is a need to balance the Project Board and there are two suppliers.

Senior Supplier – There are two major suppliers to the project and these are represented on the Project Board.

Executive – The new owner has the business interests and the accountability for the project.

Project Assurance – No one in the scenario has suitable skills to fulfil this role. It is a small project with teamwork essential. I recommend that the Project Board members undertake their own project assurances. Responsibility always rests with the Project Board.

Project Support – will be carried out by the office staff, in terms of filing and organising for configuration management. It is unlikely that they will have the skills needed to do more.

Team Managers – There are several Team Managers needed for this project. Some are external and some internal. Each major piece of work will have a Team Manager identified, as there are discrete work packages in this project. The foreman is in a position to act as Team Manager for the office design but I recommend the ship builder as Team Manager to build it.

Marker's comments

The organisation structure matches the solution held by the examiners and the above reasons were good. Note, however, that the question did not ask for reasons. Therefore just the organisation structure would have been enough to gain the marks. Only give reasons if the question asks for them. Otherwise you are wasting precious time writing words that will not earn extra marks.

Question 3(b)

Other options are to have a single Senior Supplier and Senior User (foreman and contract yacht transportation company) as they are the main risk areas in the project. A supplier group could be formed to have input from the external suppliers.

Marker's comments

Not quite certain what the first sentence means. The offered organisation only had one Senior User; the foreman, so what is the alternative? From the suggestion of foreman and contract yacht transportation company, the candidate does not mean to combine the roles. The sample answer has a suggestion that the new owner took on the Senior User role as well as Executive role. As Project Board members are supposed to be able to commit resources, the new owner may feel that only he can do this, not the foreman. When you consider who the suppliers are, it seems unlikely that they could be formed into a group. The yacht transporters, local council and electricity company seem to have little in common at a management level. It is difficult to imagine any one of these suppliers controlling the others as sub-contractors.

The Project Manager could do project support if the office staff do not have time due to the additional work involved in the move. The Project Manager could also act as Team Manager for the internal work packages. He is likely to be up to date with what is happening in each work package, as it is a small project. I do not recommend he act as Team Manager for external work packages.

It is possible to consider bringing in external Project Assurance, but with a short timeframe project in a small team who work well together, I do not recommend this additional overhead to be needed. The Project Board are likely to have the skills for both project management standards (Executive) and quality assurance (Senior User and Senior Supplier.)

Marker's comments

This seems very unlikely, and no reasons are given to suggest what skills the external Project Assurance would need to have. Would it be assurance for the Executive, i.e. someone watching the pennies, someone with logistics skills? If such a suggestion is to be made, there would have to be much more detail in terms of what assurance was to be sought.

Question 3(c)

Stages for this project need to coincide with natural decision points. Each time the Project Board meets they are tackling decisions and giving direction to the project to keep it in control.

Marker's comments

Again a general comment, not earning marks.

All projects need an initiation stage (PRINCE2 recommends it).

Marker's comments

The remark about initiation earns marks.

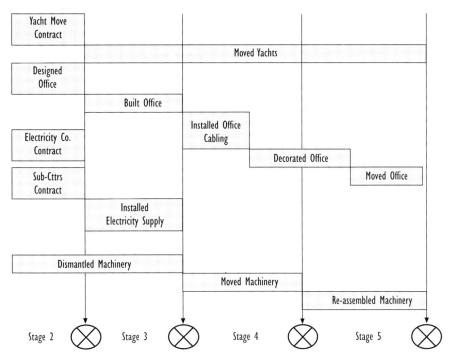

(Stage 1 = Initiation Stage)

Reasons

Stage 1 – Initiation – firm foundation

Stage 2 – Once contracts are ready, ask the Project Board (PB) to sign them off and agree the office design

Stage 3 – Once the electricity is installed and machinery is dismantled, is the PB satisfied that the new site is ready for the machinery to be moved? Has the new road been completed in time?

Stage 4 – Once the machinery is moved, is the PB satisfied it is ready for reassembly? I recommend this coincides with the first three yachts being moved prior to Xmas.

Stage 5 – Is the PB satisfied that all the yachts have been successfully moved and the new boatyard premises are fit to resume boat building?

There are frequent stages to keep under tight control, as this is a high-risk project. The stage boundaries allow PB involvement at potential risk points.

Marker's comments

There were marks available for mentioning that risk and time monitoring were major influences on stage choice, so this last sentence picked those up.

Summary: The paper would have scored very high marks – in excess of 100 out of the 150 available. There were only the small issues, pointed out in the notes, that would have missed marks. Possibly the most important observations are:

● Answer the question, not less than is requested, but equally not more

● Don't write general comments. The candidate avoided writing long essays that make it difficult for the examiner to spot items that earn marks among lots of general comments.

Close out

If you've managed to get this far you are as ready for the PRINCE2 examinations as you are ever likely to be. It remains only to wish you the little bit of luck that we all need to make a success of any venture in life. If you are still not confident of your knowledge of PRINCE2 or your ability to convince an examiner that you are able to apply it to a given situation, you should consider attending an APM Group accredited training event and, perhaps, try to gain a little more experience in using the method.

Practising writing answers to typical project management situations, using the approaches suggested in this book will certainly help to prepare you for the examination and help develop your ability to respond to a problem using a structured method.

The scenario for which the specimen answers have been prepared can also be used to practise writing further answers – for example *'Describe how you would handle any changes required during the project'* and *'Write a Product Description for one of the products in your Product Breakdown Structure'*.

You can also use your own experience to generate a scenario and questions – this is sometimes the easiest way to start your preparation. Try to identify the key topics for each question first; then answer the questions (or at least some parts of them). Remember that you will not score all the marks for just identifying and explaining the PRINCE2 topic, but that you must relate the topic to the scenario, and measure your answer against the marking scheme – this, after all, is exactly what the examiner will be doing!

Good luck with your preparation.

Ken Bradley

February 2002

Appendix: Examiners' marking guidelines

Questions

Q1(a)   Draw a Product Breakdown Structure for the specialist products for the Project Plan for the scenario (18 marks)

Q1(b)   Create a Product Flow Diagram from the Product Breakdown Structure (18 marks)

(For producing non-trivial diagrams which follow Product-based Planning principles, 14 marks)

	No. of products from scenario	Marking approach	Products Identified		
			≤6	≤10	>10
1	Genuine PBS levels	Ignore any trivial bottom levels and also any that are not carried into the PFD. 1–1 breakdowns do not count	2	3	3
2	PBS quality (no 1–1, joining up at a lower level, genuine 'consisting of', no arrows)	Basic score is the number on the left. Lose 1 mark for each error type. Score 0 if not recognisably a PBS, e.g. 50% of diagram consists of error types. The extra mark(s) on the right can be awarded for a sound diagram that obeys the rules	2–3	3–4	4–5
3	PBS–PFD match. Add 0.5 for correct transfer to max – if take-over numbers rather than names allow half available marks – so if they get some correct they get some credit	We are assessing the technique. Diagram must at least have top and lowest level products. Minimum marks available 0, i.e. no negative scores	3	5	6
4	Dependencies	Marks in proportion to the number of correct/incorrect dependencies	4	8	10
5	External products different symbol (2) correct products for their identified PBS (2)	2 for different symbol. 2 marks if all externals correct. 1 mark lost for a mixture of correct and incorrect external products	4	4	4
6	Products not activities		2	4	4
7	Scenario products in diagrams	Proportion as a total number of products shown in plan (21)	5	10	15
8	Correct breakdown/ appropriate use of intermediate prods in PFD	All marks if intermediate products not used. >1 error = no marks	2	2	3
Extras					
		Total			

Examiner's notes: Question 1(a) Product Breakdown Structure and Question 1(b) Product Flow Diagram

1   The first action is to count the number of scenario products, compared with the sample answer, that are in the answer. This indicates the column to use for the maximum number of marks available, e.g. if a diagram has only six recognisable products, the whole question is marked against column 1 where the maximum number of marks is 30.

2   The top box does not count as a level. Ignore management and quality 'legs'. Award one mark up to the maximum in the column for each breakdown. Accept a list of products at the bottom level as an extra level. If the bottom level is trivial and not carried forward into the Product Flow Diagram, ignore this as a level.

3   Deduct a mark for any example of the errors quoted. Do not deduct a further mark for a second example of the same error. At present an indented list has to be accepted as a diagram, but would not earn the extra mark.

4   Errors are PBS products not in PFD and PFD products not in PBS. Deduct a mark here if the PBS did not start and the PFD not finish with the end product. This is a mechanical exercise. Even if the PBS products are wrong, award marks if they are transferred to the PFD.

5   Award marks in the ratio of correct/incorrect dependencies in the diagram submitted by the candidate. Intermediate products that precede their lower level products in the PFD are errors.

6   For full marks the external products must appear in the Product Breakdown Structure and be in an ellipse or different symbol in the PFD. If they are in an ellipse but were not in the PBS, award only two marks. If one external has been dealt with correctly but other external products have been treated as internal ones, award only one of the two marks. Award no marks for external sources instead of products.

7   Deduct half a mark for each activity in the Product Flow Diagram up to the maximum. If there are activities in the PBS, ignore these if the candidate corrects these to products in the PFD.

8   Count the number of bottom-level products in the sample answer (12) and compare these with the number identified by the candidate. Award marks in ratio.

9   If no intermediate products used in the PFD, award all marks. Deduct a mark if there is an error in the use of intermediate PBS products in the PFD, e.g. an intermediate product precedes its lower level products in the Product Flow Diagram. If there is more than one incorrect use, award no marks.

Examiner's notes: Guideline PBS and PFD

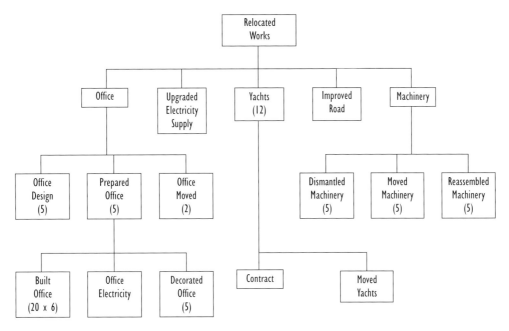

Product Breakdown Structure

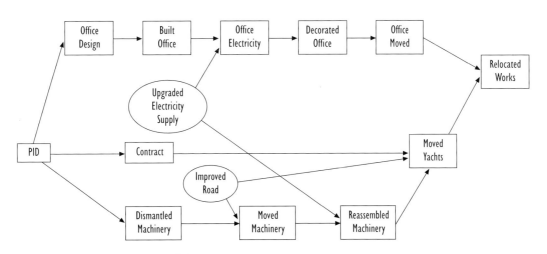

Product Flow Diagram

Questions

Q2(a)   Select three risks associated with the scenario and using the PRINCE2 approach carry out a risk evaluation (23 marks)

Q2(b)   Make proposals for the management of each risk (10 marks)

Q2(c)   Identify the major events at which the Project Manager will examine risks (17 marks)

Q2(a) Risk evaluation on three risks associated with the scenario

1	3 sensible risks identified from the scenario (2 marks for each)	6
2	1 × 3 marks for probability/impact rating (1 × 3 for reasoning)	6
3	Balance of cost of risk action(s) against cost if risk occurs (3 × 1)	3
4	Specific Actions (3 × 2)	6
5	Owners appointed	2

Q2(b) Risk Management

1	Specific actions and people for planning (2), resourcing (3), monitoring (3) and controlling (2)	10

Q2(c) Identify the major events at which the Project Manager will examine risks

6	Risk Log	1
7	SU (2) IP (2) risk activities	4
8	CS5 (2) CS6 Highlight Reporting (2)	4
9	ESA risk review	2
10	Tolerance connection (2) time is the key element (2)	4
11	Risk consideration when assessing Project Issues	2

Extras

Total

Examiner's notes: Question 2(a)

1   There are several risks made clear in the scenario, such as failure to upgrade the road in time, failure to enhance the power supply and the yacht removal company not starting on time or having its equipment break down. Award two marks for each of these or any others in the scenario. Do not award marks for any risks not contained in the scenario.

2   One mark is available for measurement of each of the three risks identified. The answer should cover both probability and impact to qualify for the mark. Award a further mark per risk if reasons are given.

3   Considered outcome of each risk carries a mark. This may be as little as answering the question 'Is it acceptable?' or may go further into the cost of taking action versus the cost of doing nothing. No marks should be awarded if the candidate uses this heading to simply list the actions to be taken.

4   Marks are available for each set of sensible responses/actions for the three risks. The responses must be specific to the scenario and the risk, rather than simply repeating the five response types. If the latter is done, a mark can be awarded.

5   Marks are available for candidates who show understanding of the need to assign an owner.

6   The candidate may have listed an owner in an evaluation matrix, identified an owner in the text or simply mentioned the general need for risk owners.

Examiner's notes: Question 2(b)

1   Each of the four elements of risk management carries marks. These should be awarded for relating the elements to the scenario and the identified risks, i.e. inserting actions into the stage plans, relating risk owner to the resourcing and monitoring, and actions that relate to the control step. Marks should be reduced if the answer is more general, down to one mark for simply mentioning the four elements.

Examiner's notes: Question 2(c)

1   Award a mark for any mention of the Risk Log.

2   Award two marks each for mentioning the risk activities in SU and IP, e.g. setting up the Risk Log, checking the Project Mandate for risks in SU, checking the Project Plan and Business Case for risks in IP.

3   Award two marks for identifying that risk status should be checked in CS5, Reviewing Stage Status. Award two marks for mentioning that the Highlight Report will contain a risk review. Award only one mark each if the candidate simply lists the process and product names.

4   Award two marks for mentioning that risks are reviewed at ESA time. Award only one mark if ESA, SB3 or DP3 or End Stage Report is mentioned without explanation.

5   Award two marks for identifying the possible impact of risk occurrence on tolerances. If the candidate identifies that time is the major risk factor in the scenario, award two extra marks.

6   Award two marks for identifying the review and possible update of the Risk Log when assessing Project Issues (CS4). Award only one mark if CS4 (Examining Project Issues) mentioned without explanation.

Questions

Q3(a)   Draw an organisation structure for the project, naming the people who would fill each role (22 marks)

Q3(b)   Explain briefly any other project organisation options that you might consider (14 marks)

Q3(c)   Suggest stages for the project and give reasons for your choice (14 marks)

Q3(a) Draw an organisation structure for the project, naming the people who would fill each role

1	New owner as Executive	4
2	Foreman as Senior User	4
3	Yacht removal firm take (part of) Senior Supplier role	3
4	Project Board would do their own assurance	4
5	Probably no need for project support (1) or help from office staff (1)	2
6	Team Managers (1) from external suppliers (2) and foreman (2)	5

Q3(b) Explain briefly any other project organisation options that you might consider

7	Several suppliers (1) including own resources (1) electricity company (1) electrician and decorator (1)	4
8	Should owner take on Senior User role/Senior Supplier role as well? (4)	3
9	Would new owner be better choice as Senior Supplier? (2) or the foreman? (2)	4
10	Should the outside contractors share Senior Supplier role?	3

Q3(c) Suggest stages for the project and give reasons for your choice

11	1 mark each for sensible specialist stage to a maximum of 5, e.g. covers all identified specialist products, matches PFD drawn, does not include project closure as a stage. 1 mark for each stage explanation up to a maximum of 3	8
12	Risk (2) and time (2) monitoring are major influences on stage choice	4
13	Recognition that PRINCE2 requires an initiation stage	2

Extras

Total

Examiner's notes: Question 3(a)

1   Don't accept anyone not mentioned in the scenario

2   Suggest the new owner as Executive. No other answer should be accepted (10 marks)

3   Suggest the foreman as Senior User (11 marks)

4   Award three marks for the removal firm as either all or part of the Senior Supplier role. Other suggestions are taken care of elsewhere.

5   Award a mark for mention of Project Assurance. Award three marks for identifying that the project is so small that the Project Board would do its own assurance. If the candidate suggests bringing in someone else, allow a mark if this is backed by a reasonable argument. Do not accept Quality Assurance instead of Project Assurance.

6   Both marks should be awarded if both suggestions are made, i.e. too small for any specialist help, but may get office staff to help with things like filing and configuration management. Award one mark for mentioning project support but not both if any specialists introduced.

7   Award one mark for mentioning Team Managers, and two further marks for identifying that external providers such as the decorating, removal and electricity firms will use this role. Two further marks are available for identifying that the foreman may act as a Team Manager.

Examiner's notes: Question 3(b)

1   Award a mark if the candidate recognises that there are several suppliers. Award extra marks for the identification of these groups.

2   Award three marks if the question of the new owner taking on the Senior User role is raised.

3   Award three marks if the candidate raises the possibility of the new owner as Senior Supplier. Award two marks if the foreman is suggested. No marks for anyone not mentioned in the scenario. No marks for an outsider in an assurance role.

4   Award up to three marks for a suggestion that the outside contractors might share the role of Senior Supplier.

Examiner's notes: Question 3(c)

1   Award up to five marks for a reasonable suggestion of stages for the project. Reduce the maximum to four marks if Project Closure is included as a stage. The suggested stages should match the PFD drawn by the candidate and include all the specialist products identified by the candidate. A sensible maximum would be around three or four stages. Reduce the marks awarded if an unreasonably high number is suggested, unless this is backed by good explanations. Award up to three more marks for explanations of why these stages were chosen.

2   Award two marks each if the candidate ties stages to the riskiness of the project and the need to keep tight control over the time element.

3   PRINCE2 says that there should be an initiation stage. Award two marks for such a suggestion.

Index